Diana
The People's Princess

Richard Wood

RSVP

RAINTREE
STECK-VAUGHN
PUBLISHERS
The Steck-Vaughn Company

Austin, Texas

A donation from the proceeds of this book will be made to the Diana, Princess of Wales, Memorial Trust.

Cover photograph: Diana sitting with a young girl who has been the victim of a land mine explosion in Angola, 1997
Title page: Diana with her sons, William and Harry, at a theme park in 1993

Published by Raintree Steck-Vaughn Publishers, an imprint of Steck-Vaughn Company

Library of Congress Cataloging-in-Publication Data
Wood, Richard.
Diana: the people's princess / Richard Wood.
   p.   cm.
   Includes bibliographical references and index.
   ISBN 0-8172-3998-7 (Hard)
   0-8172-7849-4 (Soft)
   I. Title.   II. Series.

Printed in Italy. Bound in the United States.
1 2 3 4 5 6 7 8 9 0 02 01 00 99 98

Picture acknowledgments
The publishers would like to thank the following for allowing their pictures to be reproduced in this publication: Camera Press 5 (top), 7, 9, 20, 31, 35, 38 (both), 44, 45 (top); Getty Images/Fox Photos 15; Popperfoto 12 (bottom), 13 (bottom), 14, 39, 45 (bottom); Rex Features, London *cover*, 1, 6 (both), 10, 12, 13 (top), 16, 17, 18 (both), 19, 21, 22, 23 (both), 27 (both), 28, 29, 30, 33, 36, 37, 40, 41, 42, 43; Topham Picturepoint 4, 5 (bottom), 8, 11, 24, 25, 26, 32, 34 (both).

Contents

The Spencer Family

Diana Spencer was not born a princess. She did not even become "Lady Diana" until she was 13 years old, when her grandfather died and her father became Earl Spencer. The Spencers are one of the oldest and richest families in Great Britain, and their family has lived on the same estates at Althorp in Northamptonshire for 500 years.

Diana grew to be proud of her Spencer background, but as a small child it meant little to her. Her childhood was spent at Park House in Norfolk. She loved the comfortable, rambling old house, surrounded by rolling fields and woods where she played with her two older sisters, Sarah and Jane, and her younger brother, Charles.

Baby Di. Like many upper-class babies, Diana spent more time with a succession of nannies than with her parents.

Above: *As children, Diana and her younger brother, Charles, were particularly close.*

Right: *Diana's father kept photograph albums of his children. This is Diana at seven.*

But when Diana was just seven years old, a terrible shadow was cast across her life. Her parents divorced, and her mother moved away to live in London. Diana felt abandoned and helpless. She never forgot the sound of her mother's car driving away that night. She hoped that her own children would never suffer a similar distress.

Home and School

Below: ***Diana's father, Earl Spencer, with his second wife, Raine. Diana worshiped her father and was very upset when he remarried in 1976.***

Diana's first school was in Norfolk, near her home. Though the classes were small and the teachers very caring, Diana always found school life difficult. Unlike her brother, Charles, she did not shine in her work. She became quiet and shy, though she was especially kind and helpful to younger children.

Below: ***Althorp (pronounced "all trup"), where Diana's family moved when she was 14 years old. She found it spooky, "like an old man's club, full of clocks ticking."***

When she was nine years old, Diana's father sent her away to boarding school. She did not want to leave home and complained, "If you love me, you won't leave me here!" However, she soon came to love the school, where she excelled at swimming and dancing and was awarded a prize for helpfulness. Best of all, she was allowed to have Peanuts, her pet guinea pig, with her at school.

During the school breaks at home in Park House, Diana sometimes met royalty. The queen and her family became Diana's neighbors when they stayed at nearby Sandringham, a royal residence. The younger royal children, Prince Andrew and Prince Edward, would visit the Spencers at Park House to use their private swimming pool. In return, the Spencer children were invited back to play at Sandringham.

Diana with her pony, Soufflé, in Scotland, 1974. She loved animals, but an early fall from a horse put her off riding for life.

In Diana's own words: *"I loved being at school. I was very naughty in the sense of always wanting to muck about rather than sit tight looking at the four walls of the schoolroom."*

Children's Favorite

When she was 13, Diana started at West Heath, a senior girls' boarding school in Kent. She was never a particularly good student, and Diana was keenly aware of her weak academic standing.

After leaving school, Diana moved to London to share a flat with three friends. She took a cooking course, and did housework, waitressing, and cleaning through a work agency called Solve Your Problems. She also worked as a nanny, looking after young children for wealthy London families. The children loved her. Her talents were discovered, and before long she was working as a nursery school teacher.

The teenager with the cheeky smile. Diana was often in trouble at school and was once nearly expelled for going out at night on a dare.

Voluntary Service

West Heath School's Community Service plan had a lasting effect on Diana. Every week, she cleaned and made tea for an old lady in Kent. On Tuesday evenings, she and her friends visited a local mental hospital to help look after the patients. Diana's father had once told her to treat everyone as an equal.

"Miss Diana" with children at the Young England Kindergarten. Her musical and dancing talents were much in demand in the classroom.

Royal Romance

Diana's happy-go-lucky life in London did not last long. In July 1980, when Diana was just 19 years old, she and Prince Charles were guests together at a weekend party. As they chatted, the prince, who was grieving the death of his great uncle, Lord Mountbatten, was touched by her sympathy and understanding. He invited her back to Buckingham Palace the next day. She refused—but other invitations followed, and before long a romance began to develop.

The prince had once said that 30 was the ideal age to settle down. Now he was nearly 33 and still unmarried. Newspaper stories often linked his name with other girlfriends. But when Diana began to appear at Charles's side, many people sensed that this time the Prince of Wales might be serious. There was something fresh and natural about "Lady Di," and her shy glance quickly captured everyone's hearts. To great excitement, the couple announced their engagement in February of 1981.

Once the secret was out, Diana's every movement was followed by the press.

10

Charles and Diana announce their engagement. "With Charles at my side, I cannot go wrong," she said.

In Diana's own words: "He said, 'Will you marry me?' I remember thinking, 'This is a joke,' and I said, 'Yeah, OK,' and laughed. He was deadly serious. He said, 'You do realize that one day you will be Queen.' A voice said to me inside, 'You won't be Queen, but you'll have a tough role.'"

A Fairy-tale Wedding

Returning to Buckingham Palace. The wedding was a major celebration, full of pomp and pageantry.

Charles and Diana were married on July 29, 1981. Huge crowds gathered in London along the procession route between Buckingham Palace and St. Paul's Cathedral, hoping for a glimpse of the royal couple. As the procession of carriages appeared, people cheered and waved flags. Meanwhile, 750 million people all over the world gathered in front of their television sets to watch the live broadcast.

The Archbishop of Canterbury, in his sermon, described the wedding as "the stuff of which fairy tales are made." For the public, it all seemed to go without a hitch—except, that is, when Diana repeated Prince Charles's first names in the wrong order. She was very nervous, as anyone would be.

In private, though, Diana was in distress. After the engagement, she had moved into Buckingham Palace to learn "how" to become a princess. But life there seemed strange, cold, and unfriendly. She was regularly sick with an illness called bulimia nervosa and lost a lot of weight. She missed the fun and freedom of her old life with her friends. Surely, she hoped, things would improve once the wedding was over.

A small selection of the many souvenirs that people bought to help them remember this very special day

On the balcony at Buckingham Palace. "Give her a kiss," people shouted, and the prince, eventually, did.

Shy Di

With her marriage to Prince Charles, Diana ceased to be "Lady Diana." She was now "Her Royal Highness the Princess of Wales."

In a very short time, and at only 20, she had to adapt to married life while learning to be royal herself. Despite her privileged upbringing, it was not easy. With her naturally shy personality, she was sometimes upset by the mass of journalists and cameramen who followed her everywhere she went.

The royal couple in Australia on their first major overseas tour. Diana was constantly surprised by how many people would turn out to see her.

Grand formal occasions, such as palace dinners for important visitors, could be even more terrifying. Diana had a great deal to learn. On one occasion, she did not know who the gentleman sitting opposite her was. "That," said her husband, "is the Chancellor of Germany, one of the most powerful men in the world."

Diana felt more relaxed on visits like this, to the Great Ormond Street Hospital for Sick Children in London. She tried hard to ignore the constant flashes of cameras behind her.

A Princess in the Kitchen

Diana often felt uneasy with royal guests. It is said that at Balmoral, the queen's Scotland home, she used to hang around the kitchens talking to the staff instead. A servant once pointed to the door and said, "Through there, Ma'am, is your side of the house; through here is our side."

Royal Roles

Despite her shyness, Princess Diana was eager to start work as a member of the royal family. She began to go on royal visits with Prince Charles. "I wanted us to share everything together. I thought that we were a very good team," she said. But wherever they went, it was Diana the people cheered and Prince Charles was left collecting flowers to pass on to her.

The prince and princess at one of Charles's polo matches. "We make a good team," she said.

The royal family had done much work for charity for a long time. Somehow, though, they still seemed remote from ordinary people's problems. Diana was different. She took a sincere personal interest in those she met. Polite handshakes were not enough for her; she longed to touch people and was not afraid to hold hands and hug those in distress. This was Diana's special gift, and people loved her for it. As an Australian later said, "She was the human face of royalty."

Of all her duties, it was visits like this, to a school for disabled children, that meant most to Diana.

In Diana's own words: "I remember when I used to sit on hospital beds and hold people's hands. People used to be sort of shocked because they said they'd never seen this before. To me it was quite a normal thing to do."

Motherhood

Princess Diana's father once said, "It will be a lucky baby who has Diana as a mother." There was not long to wait. Prince William was born in June 1982, and Prince Harry was born two years later.

Of all the roles Diana took on, being a good mother was by far the most important to her. Remembering her own unhappy childhood, she promised never to let her children feel unwanted. When she and Prince Charles were due to leave for a tour of Australia, she refused to go without Prince William. This was unheard of for the royal family, but Diana got her way.

Below: **June 1989, and a barefoot Diana wins the mothers' race at Wetherby School, which Princes William and Harry attended.**

Above: **Diana proudly leaves the hospital with newborn Prince Harry, September 1984.**

Other royal mothers may have been affectionate with their children in private, but Diana loved to hug them in public. "Cuddles have no nasty side effects," she said.

As much as possible, Diana wanted her children to live normal lives. She chose schools that were near home so that she could join in parents' activities with the other mothers. Dressed in jeans and sneakers, the boys went with her to theme parks and to see the latest movies. Once William, the future king, was in his teens, Diana discussed everything with him. It was his idea for her to sell many of her dresses to raise money for charity.

Diana was always game for a laugh with her sons. They all enjoyed the water ride at a theme park in 1993.

The Hidden Pain

To many people, Princess Diana's life must have seemed magical. She appeared to have everything anyone could wish for—beauty, wealth, popularity, two lovely children, and a caring husband.

In Diana's own words: "Bulimia is like a secret disease. You inflict it upon yourself because you don't think you're worthy or valuable. You fill your stomach up four or five times a day, and it gives you a feeling of comfort."

Princess Diana had a remarkable ability to cover up her sorrow in public. But sometimes, however hard she tried, her true feelings showed through.

But secretly, Diana was suffering. After both her children were born, she suffered from depression, which leaves new mothers feeling very tired and unhappy. No one else in the royal family had suffered from this problem, and they seemed unable to understand or help. Despite her busy and glamorous lifestyle, Diana often felt lonely.

It seemed to Diana that, however hard she tried, no one close to her ever thanked her for her hard work. She began to feel rejected, just as she had as a child. Diana also felt that she was growing apart from her husband. Her eating disorder returned and she became very thin. People noticed, and the newspapers began to hint that something was seriously wrong with her life.

By 1992, the distance between Charles and Diana was plain for all to see. She always found formal events, like this, particularly difficult.

21

The Princess and the Press

However awful Diana felt privately, she knew that she could not display her emotions. She quickly learned to cover up her inner feelings with an amazing show of happiness. The press loved her, and she was treated like a movie star. Diana was the most photographed woman in the world.

Diana arriving for a movie premiere with Sir Richard Attenborough. Attenborough, a famous actor and director, coached Diana in public speaking to help her with her charity work.

Diana's tall, graceful figure stood out in a crowd whatever she wore. She had a perfect sense of style and knew how important it was to look just right for every occasion. Her specially designed dresses became famous, and much copied, the world over. Magazines competed to see who could get the best pictures of Diana, knowing that a good picture of her would sell thousands of extra copies.

At times, all this attention became too much for Diana. She tried to persuade photographers not to pursue her. When that did not work, she tried to shake them off, slipping out of back doors, hiding her face behind bags, and driving off at high speed. But Diana knew that she could never entirely escape their attention. Nor did she always wish to—she depended on the press to publicize her charity work.

Right: *June 1997, at London's Royal Albert Hall for a concert. With good reason, Diana was often called "the world's most beautiful woman."*

23

The Marriage Breaks Down

By the early 1990s, Diana was showing the strains of ten years in the spotlight. There were many rumors about a breakdown in her marriage to Prince Charles. The couple seemed to spend less and less time together. Prince Charles was said to have renewed his friendship with a former girlfriend, Camilla Parker-Bowles, while Diana's name was linked with various other men. When Charles and Diana made a visit to Korea in 1992, they both looked miserable.

The prince and princess stand at attention at the National Cemetery in Seoul, South Korea, November 1992. This was their final tour together.

24

The Queen was worried, too. Most of the newspaper reports were based on guesswork and were often untrue. However, it was obvious that relations between the prince and princess were bad, and this was harming the popularity of the rest of the royal family. For Diana, who remembered the pain of her own parents' divorce, it was a personal disaster. Yet she agreed, reluctantly, to accept a formal separation from Prince Charles in December 1992.

How British newspapers announced the separation of Charles and Diana, December 10, 1992. Diana described it as the saddest day of her life.

Going Public

Separated from Prince Charles, Diana perhaps hoped for a more normal life. This was not to be. The public's interest in her was as great as ever, and journalists still would not leave her alone. At times, she felt as if she were a prisoner in her own home, unable to do or say anything without being criticized.

Some of Prince Charles's friends blamed Diana for the separation and hinted publicly that she was mentally ill. In fact, she was feeling stronger than ever, having at last conquered her eating problems.

Diana determined to fight back. Working through friends, she had already helped journalist Andrew Morton write a book, *Diana, Her True Story*, to tell her side of events. Overnight, the book became a best-seller. Later, she gave a television interview speaking about her life, her troubles, her ideas about royalty, and her hopes for her children. The royal family was horrified by the program, but she won the sympathy and affection of millions.

Author Andrew Morton with his book, based on information from Diana and her friends

Left: **On a visit to India with Prince Charles in 1990, Diana chose to pose alone in front of the Taj Mahal. It was through pictures like this without Charles that the public was first made aware of her unhappiness.**

Right: **In 1995, Diana was interviewed by Martin Bashir on television. The program was kept secret until it was about to be shown.**

The Belle of the Ball

Princess Diana loved all types of music. She had played the piano since childhood and could entertain the crew of the Royal Yacht to a lively evening's musicmaking. Her tastes ranged from the solemn tones of Verdi's *Requiem* to the latest songs by her friend Elton John.

As a girl, Diana had hoped to be a ballet dancer, but grew too tall—"I overshot the mark," she said. Of the charities she helped, the English National Ballet was especially close to her heart. She became their Founder Patron in 1989 and over the next eight years made hundreds of visits to performances given by the dance company.

Dancing with actor John Travolta at the White House in 1985. "For fifteen minutes, she made me feel like a prince. It was absolutely magical," he said.

With dancers of the English National Ballet for a gala performance of Swan Lake, 1997

Diana was involved in every aspect of the ballet's work—from raising funds to choosing costumes and repertoire and looking after the welfare of the dancers. As with all her charity work, she did far more behind the scenes than was ever known to the public.

The Dancers' Inspiration

"When Diana came here, she always radiated a warmth, a grace, a happiness and a beauty—all things which are particularly special to dancers. She was completely at ease with the dancers, and they were inspired by her."
—Jim Fletcher, English National Ballet.

29

Children's Champion

Diana was so popular with the public that more and more organizations asked her for help. Over the years, she agreed to be patron or president of nearly a hundred charities. Patrons normally just attend occasional dinners and lend support to appeals. But Diana was different. She wanted to find out all about her charities and to meet the staff and the people they helped. Though she was always nervous about speaking in public, she took lessons so she would be more comfortable. She wrote her own speeches, and spoke movingly in support of many good causes.

The chance to sit on the princess's knee brings a smile to the face of a young leukemia patient.

30

Diana loved to visit children in hospitals and often did so unannounced. One girl said, "I shall always remember her eyes—they were so beautiful, like the rest of her."

Children's charities were especially close to Diana's heart. Barnardo's helps tens of thousands of young people and their families, especially those with special needs and those suffering from poverty and abuse. When the princess became president of the charity in 1984, she became actively involved. By 1996, she had attended 110 events as well as making many private visits to see the charity's work for herself.

My Smiling Friend

Eight-year-old Danielle Stephenson, who has a rare heart problem, first met Diana when the princess stopped in for a regular visit to the Royal Brompton Hospital. When she was well enough, Diana invited Danielle back to Kensington Palace for tea, and gave her a gold chain with a letter "D" on it, like the one she had owned. For Danielle, Diana was "the friend who always left us smiling."

Being Herself

After Diana separated from Prince Charles, there were fewer royal duties for her to perform. This gave Diana the chance, which she had long wanted, to do more charity work.

To begin with, she tried to support all the charities of which she was a patron. But with so many appeals for help, it was impossible to give them all the time and attention they deserved. In 1996, she reluctantly gave up being a patron of all but six charities. At last she was able to concentrate on the issues that most concerned her.

At London's Great Ormond Street Hospital for Sick Children, 1997. Diana often followed up her visits to sick children by sending letters, cards, and presents.

Always a regular hospital visitor, Diana was sometimes moved to tears by the sight of young children in pain. Both of her own sons had been patients at the Great Ormond Street Hospital for Sick Children. Diana not only helped raise huge sums of money for the hospital ($85 million in only two years) but she was a regular visitor, too.

Diana's presence always had a wonderful effect on children. One mother recalled, "During the time she spent with us, it was clear that to her nothing else in the world mattered. Her warmth helped us to smile again."

Diana showed her deep compassion by wrapping her arms round people and hugging them.

On the Streets

Left: *In March 1997, Diana met Dave and Portia while visiting Centrepoint's cold weather project in King's Cross, London. The shelter provides food, beds, and help for 47 homeless young people.*

As Diana drove around London, she was often sad to see people begging on the streets or sleeping outside in bad weather in doorways and under bridges. During the 1980s and 1990s, many people had enjoyed opportunities and riches like never before. But this was another side of life, largely hidden from view, one that Diana was determined to tell people about.

Right: *Diana speaking on behalf of the Centrepoint charity, 1995. Though she never felt at ease speaking in public, she knew how much good her words could do.*

Diana was horrified to find some people as young as 11 sleeping on the streets.

Centrepoint

To the end of her life, Diana worked for Centrepoint, a charity that helps homeless young people. Diana liked their positive approach, providing hostels and food, but also helping homeless people find permanent homes and work.

As in all her work, the princess became involved with helping people in private as well as in public. Often she would secretly slip out of her Kensington Palace home and visit night shelters for homeless people. Sometimes she took Prince William and Prince Harry along too, to chat or play cards with the people there. "I want them to have an understanding of people's feelings, people's distress, and people's hopes," she said.

A Helping Hand

Some charities are more well known than others and are therefore easier to raise money for. But Diana, typically, went out of her way to support the less-known causes that are usually ignored.

Cancer and AIDS are diseases that many people do not even like to think about. They cause great pain, not only to sufferers but to friends who helplessly watch people die slowly. As president of the Royal Marsden Trust Cancer Hospital, Diana regularly comforted dying people. By auctioning 79 of her dresses in June 1997, she raised almost $5 million to help patients.

Diana comforts an AIDS patient at the Middlesex Hospital, July 1991. She was a good listener and seemed instinctively to know how other people felt.

Diana first become involved with AIDS ten years earlier. At that time, many people refused to touch AIDS sufferers, afraid they might catch the virus. Diana not only touched them, she warmly held hands and hugged them. Her concern with AIDS became very personal when she helped nurse a friend, Adrian Ward-Jackson, through the last months of his life. She took Prince William to see him and flew to be with Adrian when he died. As so often, people's attitudes toward AIDS changed because of Diana's involvement.

In Diana's own words: "I would like to be a Queen in people's hearts ... someone's got to go out there and love people, and show it."

Diana's gentle touch brought joy to people of all ages. For eleven years she was patron of the charity Help the Aged.

International Action

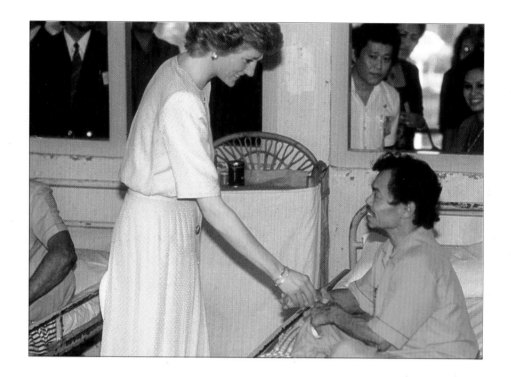

Left: *Shaking hands with a leprosy victim. Pictures like this helped educate people about the disease.*

In her last few years, Diana began to take a lead in worldwide humanitarian issues. She had often been moved by the desperate conditions of people she met on her foreign travels. Now she knew how she could help.

Bottom: *Serving bean stew to refugees in Zimbabwe, 1993.*

After visiting a hospital in Indonesia, she became a patron of the Leprosy Mission. This Christian charity treats and cares for people with leprosy in developing countries. Leprosy is a terrible disease, causing deformity and blindness. But it can be cured if caught soon enough. Many people fear the disease, and sufferers are often rejected, even by their own families.

Diana helped raise funds at home and visited leprosy hospitals in Mozambique, Nepal, and India. Photographs of her, the most glamorous woman in the world, shaking hands with sufferers helped dispel forever the myths about leprosy. In December 1996, she was awarded the "Humanitarian of the Year" award in New York City "for her work with the ill, the suffering, and the downtrodden."

Diana had a lifelong admiration for Mother Teresa. This was the last time they met, in New York City in June 1997.

Mother Teresa Meets Diana

Diana and Mother Teresa were different, yet when they met in Calcutta, India, they shared a common love of poor and outcast people. Mother Teresa once told Diana, "To heal other people you have to suffer yourself." When Diana died, Mother Teresa described her as "a very great friend who was in love with the poor."

Explosive Issues

With the divorce from Prince Charles finalized in 1996, Diana lost the title "Her Royal Highness," and became officially "Diana, Princess of Wales." But in some ways, the last few months of Diana's life were among the busiest, and perhaps the happiest, of her life. She seemed to radiate a new energy, enthusiasm, and joy.

Diana's wish to become a "humanitarian ambassador" was being taken seriously by Great Britain's prime minister, Tony Blair. And she had a new cause to fight for—land mines. An estimated 100 million land mines are scattered across sixty countries. Nobody knows exactly where. But every fifteen minutes innocent victims, mostly women and children, are killed or suffer terrible injuries from exploding mines.

Wearing protective clothing, Diana walks through a minefield in Angola. Some people criticized her for meddling in politics. "I am not a political figure," she said. "I come with my heart."

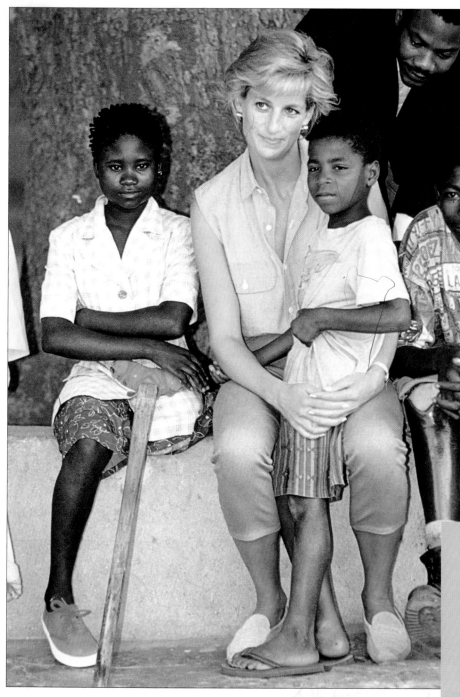

Diana was shocked by the terrible injuries she saw in Angola and Bosnia. Working a 15-hour day, she insisted on spending at least 30 minutes with every victim she met.

In January 1997, Diana visited Angola as a Red Cross volunteer to find out more about the problem. The photographs of her walking across a minefield brought the horror home to the whole world. In August she went to Bosnia. There she met victims and urged the world's governments to ban mines forever. Sadly, it was to be her last mission.

In Bosnia

"One boy took off his boots to show what his feet looked like. But he didn't have any feet left. Diana picked him up in her arms. There were no photographers there. She was not showing off. It was genuine impulse … instinctive."—Lord Deedes

A Tragic End

By August 1997, Princess Diana had at last put all her personal sorrows behind her. Following her trip to Bosnia, she was about to launch a new international campaign against land mines. Then she went on vacation with her new friend Dodi Fayed. People talked of a possible romance. Would Diana remarry? Was this her chance to move abroad, as she had often wished, and live in the United States with Dodi? We shall never know.

On Sunday, August 31, people awoke to incredible news. Diana, Dodi, and their driver had been killed in a terrible car crash in Paris. All over the world, stunned families stared in disbelief at their television screens as the details began to emerge.

To the end, Diana was hunted by the press. Here they caught up with her while on vacation with Dodi Fayed a few days before their deaths.

Diana had spent a last evening with Dodi before preparing to fly back to be with her sons. As the couple left the hotel where they had dined together, they were pursued at high speed by a group of photographers on motorcycles. As the car entered a tunnel in the city center, the driver lost control and the car crashed into a concrete pillar. The driver and Dodi were killed instantly, Diana's bodyguard was seriously hurt, and Diana herself was rushed to the hospital with massive chest injuries. In the early hours of Sunday morning, she died.

The tangled wreckage of the car in which Diana and Dodi died. Though the driver had been drinking, exactly what caused the crash may never be known.

The World Mourns

People who never met Diana felt as if they had lost a close friend. For sixteen years, she had appeared almost daily in the newspapers and on television. Diana had become, as no one else before, a part of everyone's lives. Men, women, and children openly broke down and cried. Never before had there been such public grief.

The royal family stayed at Balmoral, their Scottish home, helping the young princes come to terms with their mother's death. Plans for the funeral were made and remade as the monarchy tried to stay in tune with public feeling. On television the Queen described Diana as "an exceptional and gifted human being." Diana's death, even more than her life, may have changed the role of royalty forever.

Princess Diana's coffin enters Westminster Abbey followed by (left to right) Prince Charles, Prince Harry, Diana's brother, Charles, Prince William, and the Queen's husband, the Duke of Edinburgh.

Above: *A sea of flowers placed in front of Kensington Palace, where Diana's apartment had been. So many people wished to place tributes that thousands of flowers had to be specially flown into Great Britain.*

The following Saturday, millions lined the London streets or gathered together to watch the funeral on television. Diana's brother, Charles, described his sister as "the unique, the complex, the extraordinary, and irreplaceable Diana, whose beauty, both external and internal, will never be extinguished from our minds." The crowds outside began to applaud. Soon the congregation inside took up the applause. No one had ever applauded at a funeral before. But then no one before had ever seen the likes of Diana.

Right: *Her final resting place. Princess Diana is buried on an island in the lake at Althorp House, the ancestral home of the Spencer family.*

Glossary

AIDS Acquired Immune Deficiency Syndrome, a virus that keeps the body from resisting illnesses.

Ambassador Someone who represents a country abroad.

Auctioning Selling to whoever will pay the most.

Boarding school A school where the pupils live and study during term times.

Bulimia nervosa An illness when people overeat and then make themselves sick.

Community service A plan for giving unpaid help to local people.

Deformity Misshapen from injury or illness.

Developing countries Poor countries whose industries are still growing.

Dispel Get rid of.

Estates Lands and farms.

Extinguished Put out like a light, gotten rid of.

Formal separation An agreement, made by law, to live apart.

Glamorous Smart, rich, and exciting.

Humanitarian Done for the good of human beings.

Instinctively Done without thinking.

Leprosy Disease of the nerves and skin, causing skin to harden.

Leukemia A disease of the blood, which can cause death.

Monarchy Royalty, the royal family.

Political To do with politics or the running of a country.

Pomp and pageantry Dignified, showy events, like processions.

Sermon A short talk during a church service.

Unannounced Without anybody knowing in advance.

Upper class Having the highest status in society.

Work agency A business that helps people find work in areas that they like.

Further Information

Books

Giff, Patricia Reilly. *Diana: Twentieth Century Princess* (Women of Our Time). New York: Puffin Books, revised 1997.

Graham, Tim. *Diana, Princess of Wales: A Tribute*. International Book Marketing, 1997.

Harner, Matina, and Kristine Brennan. *Lady Diana Spencer, Princess of Wales, Philanthropist* (Women of Achievement). New York: Chelsea House, 1998.

Morton, Andrew. *Diana: In Her Own Words*. New York: Simon and Schuster, 1997.

O'Mara, Michael, editor. *Diana, Princess of Wales: A Tribute in Photographs*. New York: St. Martin's Press, 1997.

Seward, Ingrid. *Diana: An Intimate Portrait 1961–1997*. Chicago: Contemporary Books, 1997.

Spoto, Donald. *Diana: The Last Year*. New York: Harmony Books, 1997.

Videos

Diana: A Celebration, The People's Princess. Twayne Publishers, 1997.

Diana: 1961–1997. Legacy of a Princess. MPI Home Video, 1997.

Diana: Princess of Wales, The Final Farewell. ABC MPI Home Video, 1998.

Audio CD

Diana: Princess of Wales: A Tribute. New York: Bantam Books/Audio.

Important Dates

1961 Diana Spencer born at Park House, Sandringham, Norfolk.

1968 Her parents divorce.

1974 Becomes "Lady Diana" when her grandfather dies.

1979 Works as nanny and nursery teacher in London.

1981 Marries Prince Charles and becomes Princess of Wales.

1982 Prince William born.

1984 Prince Harry born.

1989 Holds hands with leprosy victims in Indonesia.

1990 Photographed looking sad and lonely while in India.

1992 Andrew Morton publishes *Diana: Her True Story*.
Diana agrees to a formal separation from Prince Charles.

1995 Gives TV interview on *Panorama*.

1996 Divorced from Prince Charles.
Decides to concentrate on six charities.
Given the "Humanitarian of the Year" Award in New York.

1997 Visits Angola and Bosnia for the landmines campaign.
Killed with Dodi Fayed in a car crash in Paris.

Index

Numbers in **bold** refer to pictures as well as text